Introduction to *The Harmonist at Nightfall*

"I want to know these scoured rocks," poet Shari Wagner writes, "the way a blind woman knows her house, / understand their journey, listen / to the creak of a glacier beneath the crust." And so begins the travels of a gifted poet as she explores the landscape and legends of Indiana with careful and loving attention, looking for and finding the universal and finally the eternal in the particular. In these poems, as Wagner takes us deeper into the natural and cultural history of this place, we become more attuned to its texture and richness. We begin to understand this house and its journey through time.

The Harmonist at Nightfall is divided into six sections. Wagner begins with poems that celebrate the natural world, a stance she never abandons. Deeply observant, Wagner lets us see how a waterfall is "iridescent / as the pearly valves of unhinged / mussels . . . / blazing like bees" or shows us in section four how a buckeye tree "drips / with April blossoms, the milk glass / chips of old chimes. In autumn, / it drops its spiny pods and turns / the color of rust on a tractor / left for decades in the rain." In later sections she explores places associated with people: The House of the Singing Winds, home of T. C. Steele; utopian founder George Rapp's Harmonie, Indiana; and Fairmount, Indiana, site of James Dean's frequently visited grave. "Where is the boy?" Wagner asks and says to the visitors to Dean's grave: "He's not here." They should look for him in the "pounding ground with the beat / of rain" where perhaps "he's riding hell-bent / over harrowed earth, stirring up dust. Or just / look for him in the solitary frame / of a farmer, shoulders slouched, hands / in his pockets, his worn boots scuffing / the crusted snow."

Later, the poems move us back in the house of history to Tippecanoe and Maconaquah (Frances Slocum), to cities lost beneath reservoirs and land lost to sinkholes, to people and centuries lost to memory: stories of the Amish, to fin de siècle and modern Indianapolis. Finally, in her journey, Wagner leaves us with Sylvan Springs. Sylvan Springs: literally an endangered architectural site in Indiana, it is mined by the poet for its deeper meaning of the spiri or deity of the forest. And this is where Wagner circles back to ete nity. "Today is a church / with its door left ajar," Wagner writes, ar she speaks of her Mennonite grandfather for whom "the psalm that moved him to prayer / rose from a wayward creek / the col of molasses."

This book you're holding represents years' worth of di pline and labor, of time and travel and, as you'll discover, the pure

joy of attention and love of language. The thing that makes a poet undertake a particular project is a mystery, finally. One day Shari Wagner was called to understand something, and the journey she decided to take was a meditative one, through the labyrinth of nature and time in a particular place in this world. The result is a gift, this collection of poems. I don't know of a writer, with the exceptions of Gene Stratton-Porter (the subject of several of these poems) or Jessamyn West, who has written with as much care and specificity of Indiana's natural beauty as Wagner does in this book. When Wagner sees an oriole at 10 o'clock in a tree she writes that "it's like opening / the tab on an advent calendar." I can't think of a better description of the experience of reading these poems.

—Susan Neville, author of *Sailing the Inland Sea: On Writing, Literature, and Land*

The Harmonist at Nightfall

Poems of Indiana

Shari Wagner

For Barbara,
a fellow Hoosier poet
Shari Wagner

Harmony Series
Bottom Dog Press

Huron, Ohio

Bottom Dog Press, Inc.
ISBN 978-1-933964-72-0
Bottom Dog Publishing
PO Box 425
Huron, Ohio 44839
http://smithdocs.net
e-mail: Lsmithdog@smithdocs.net

CREDITS:

General Editor: Larry Smith
Layout & Design: Susanna Sharp-Schwacke
Cover Design: Susanna Sharp-Schwacke
Photographs: Shari Wagner

ACKNOWLEDGMENTS

Special thanks to a Creative Renewal Fellowship from the Arts Council of Indianapolis, with funding from the Lilly Endowment, and to Individual Artist Grants from the Indiana Arts Commission, with the support of The National Endowment for the Arts. These awards covered travel expenses and allowed time for writing.

I am deeply appreciative of those who provided advice as I worked on this book. My husband, Chuck Wagner, commented on multiple drafts of all of these poems; Karen Kovacik read an earlier version of this book in manuscript form; and Gaye McKenney offered feedback on many individual poems. I would also like to thank members of my two monthly writers groups who shared revision suggestions: Ryan Ahlgrim, Rod Deaton, Dan Hess, Barbara Koons, Elizabeth Krajeck, Amy Locklin, Bonnie Maurer, Martha Maust, Nancy Pulley, Catherine Swanson and Elizabeth Weber. Finally, thanks to my editor, Larry Smith, of Bottom Dog Press for his valuable counsel and to all those who, after learning of my project, directed me toward some of their favorite Indiana parks or historical places.

Acknowledgments continued on page 111.

Contents

DEDICATION

For those who walked these trails with me,
from Angel Mounds to Devil's Backbone:

my husband, Chuck
daughters, Vienna and Iona
parents, Gerald and Mary

"This spot where you sit is your own spot.
It is on this very spot and in this very moment
that you can become enlightened.
You don't have to sit beneath a special tree
in a distant land."

—Thich Nhat Hanh

CALLING THE CROWS

Pioneer Mothers Memorial Forest
~For Vienna

We were surveying great walnut trees,
measuring ourselves against their girth,
when we heard a few caws
in the yellow canopy of leaves.
You tried to answer, but your cry
was too petite, pitched too high.

"This is how you do it," I said
and cawed like a crone—guttural, fierce.

Something in that coarse call took hold
and shook hundreds of crows
from their branches. They screamed—
a raucous chorus of harpies, wheeling
and diving above our heads, roiling
in a reckless spiral, the shape
of a trickster's warning
or its blessing—
maybe it was both.

We met each other's eyes—
not mother and daughter
but woman to woman—caught
in that vortex
of black wings and sunlight.

ONE / CIRCLING BACK

THE SOLOIST

Angel Mounds

Each morning he mounted
the slope to sing the sun
over the Ohio and past
the wild grapevines
where shy catbirds hid
and even a god
could get lost in the tangle.

He sang till yellow-rumped
warblers and mockingbirds
joined him, till the pecan grove
slid from the blue husk
of its shadow, till the wattle
and daub houses flushed
the sky's rose-mallow.

He sang as if even the hominy
cold in its pot needed
one man waking up
in the dark, one voice
striking its flint
and fanning the flame.

WINTER SOLSTICE

Mounds State Park

On the greenish-gray river
edged by ice, over the swell
of small rapids,

bundled in pelts, bringing
effigies of what traversed
the night sky—bears, serpents and birds—

up this steep bluff, a hundred
years before Christ, when there were
no trees to encumber, no junked

cars at their back, just the rush
of White River, the stark
cry of a jay some child answered,

between earthen walls when the sky
broke clear or hardened with clouds
like the surface of ice,

into a basin silent as shadows of elk
upon snow, with words that rose
in the smoke of their fires,

the Adena came to ease the frail sun
into its pallet: dirt, stone, furred
moss, the mound of their own beds.

THESE ROCKS

Turkey Run State Park

I want to know these scoured rocks
the way a blind woman knows her house,
understand their journey, listen

to the creak of a glacier beneath the crust.
I want to open the door for a pileated
woodpecker, catch splintering

water as it falls, sleep beneath the hush
of hemlocks cresting the gorge and sense
in their darkness the absent

river's surge. I want to feel the continent
shift, see orchids as snow falls,
then sink into pouches of jewelweed

filling Gypsy Gulch with a ginger glow.
I want to track wild turkeys
as they winter in Box Canyon, bend

low before their rafter of wings,
meet palm to palm my own blood brother
in iron stains leaching from stone.

CATARACT FALLS

It rumbles like a billion bison
over the brink and into a froth
of trumpeter swans. It leaps

to lash the air with puma paws,
splash rocks, iridescent
as the pearly valves of unhinged

mussels, then it dangles
in droplets, blazing like bees
or brilliant blue butterflies.

It falls as the parakeets fell,
long-tailed and fluttering
through Indiana's thick forest

before it hisses into Mill Creek
like the last massasauga
or prophecy of an old man

as he peers into the fire.

INSIDE STONE

Bluespring Caverns

The farmer never suspected
that what he fenced in
was the surface of something larger
till that morning in the early
1940s, after a thunderstorm
when he couldn't find his cows.
The pond where they'd jostle
to drink was an empty basin
he pondered with hands shoved
deep into his pockets. On the bared
slope, he spied a sinkhole,
and his lantern swept the vaulted
cavern, the cut of a subterranean
river that coursed for miles
with no one watching. It wound
past rock with velvet folds—
like the dress a girl once wore,
a stranger held at a winter dance,
her hair still damp with snow
and brown eyes clear as the water's
depth. Did they kiss beneath the mistletoe
or was it a dream plowed under
till it came out right? Waist-deep
in a loneliness he'd never known
was there, he called his black-hooved
Jerseys and heard in the distance
what might have been their bells.

CLIFTY FALLS

Only when we abandoned
the search for thundering
water, did etchings
of lotus leaves emerge
on the gray faces of shale.

We traced their veins,
then the blues of a butterfly—
coastal waters deepening
to black. The brief span
of life sunned itself
on a mossy ledge, wings
opening and closing,
silent as gills.

A million years rushed over us
in the froth of a dream
almost remembered,
stone after stone carrying us
home through the dusk.

CIRCLING BACK

Hemlock Cliffs

I've listened to this banter, this
sift of yellow ash leaves, and my feet
have sought these footholds; my fingers,
this pockmarked face.

Did I come with buckskinned pilgrims
ten thousand years ago or was it
in a dream to this box canyon
where the trailhead meets its end?

I sense the cavern's breadth
before we turn the bend. It sweeps
beneath the sandstone ridge
like a mountain lion's open maw.

If I have stood where I pause now,
watching sunlight shift the cave
from reddish-clay to umber,
maybe you came here, too.

Maybe we sat together on this
broken slab of stone while lightning
flashed spears and thunder
shook the afternoon.

OLIN LAKE

Behind us, the channel half-clogged
by bullhead lilies slips back
into the smoke of yellow tamaracks
clouding the shore. We glide
on the silk of a dream so deep, herring
break the surface from eighty feet below.

I am this hand skimming the water.
I am these eyes dazzled by light.

I am you whom I loved
before the continents were parted.

I am in the creak of wood,
old harmony of oars.

HALL WOODS

~For Chuck on our 25th anniversary

We should be shouldering
the drear weight of January,

but in this wetland forest, ferns
curl May-green amid mulch

and each oak flaunts a furry
hoof of moss. We're struck

by the surge of wind with riffled water,
the blending of worlds—voluptuous

old hills, stock-still, yet melting
into floodplain. At the brink

of Big Walnut Creek, a swift
current matches nimbus clouds.

Heaven and earth are here, my love,
passing us like herds at a gallop.

SHADES OF DEATH STATE PARK

We could be pilgrims working our way
to heaven, but there's no Elysian Field on the map,
no shelter along Sugar Creek where we might lay
our walking sticks down. Shaky ladders
lead to rugged trails and a chain of consequence:
Hemlock Hill, Devil's Punchbowl, the crumbly
bluff of Lover's Leap. Who would guess
"moderate" Kickapoo Ravine plunges
toward icy mud we scramble to evade, stumbling
through the sift of last autumn's leaves? Dark
and crisp as cinders, they succumb to an earthen
bed before wafting back to branches. Clouds shift
and sunlight turns the haunted foliage into bluebirds.

Rapture

Jasper-Pulaski Wildlife Area
~*After William Carlos Williams*

They bugle from their
breastbones and bow
to their partners, flaunt

seven-foot wingspans,
launch outlandish leaps.
They tip back

ruddy foreheads, open
beaks as if to
guzzle a bitter but

potent brew. As sunrise
drains from frosted grass,
sandhill cranes pump wings,

extend necks forward,
legs back. Like
rollicking peasants,

we could kick up
our heels and cry,
"Oya!"

But instead of round
and round, we turn
like sober pilgrims

back to our cars.

HESITATION POINT

Brown County State Park

Below us, in the forest, walnuts
are falling. Each thump, a drumbeat

or amplified heartbeat, under
yellow and Tuscan red hills.

Let's enter that pulse
on a slick ravine, past fissured

trunks and spleenwort ferns
doused in lime-green light.

Let's stop driving from vista
to vista, snapping scenic

foliage with a cell phone. Let's
trace the parched vein

of a creek bed where crayfish
hide in mud-daubed kivas, stub

our toes on half-buried geodes,
catch our breath on a stone

foundation of a house
engulfed by blazing sumac.

Let's wait, stock-still,
for the barred owl

that calls in the darkness
long after we are gone.

THE BIRDERS OF COOL CREEK

Come snow-glare or storm-light,
come swaths of gold to shift
through leaves, come mist to cleave
to mud, these Saturday morning
pilgrims keep to trails hemmed
by Walmart and Discount
Tires. Through traffic drone
they discern the chirp of a yellow-
rumped warbler and a solitary
vireo's snippet of song. The hint
of a hermit thrush, a few flute-like
trills, pulls them into a quiescent hush
until the white-throated sparrow
quickens the air. They speak
of children balancing jobs,
a flooded basement, a home
on the market, yet they glimpse
high in the sycamore, an oriole's
faint flicker. "Find ten o'clock
in that small tree," they say, patiently
pointing me to the ruby-crowned kinglet
in all that densely dappled green.
When I find him, it's like opening
the tab on an advent calendar,
the distinctive eye-ring and hidden
crown, modest herald of a forgotten
world where red-berried bushes
are beaded with the day's first light.

Two / House of the Singing Winds

THE NATURALIST

Wildflower Woods
~In memory of Gene Stratton-Porter

Two stone owls stand guard
on puddingstone posts.
Through rain and fog
their round eyes watch
for the joggle of oil lamps
and the figure of Gene, buckled
in high rubber waders,
packing a camera, a tripod
and ladders.

The arbor's flagstone path,
its twisted wisteria walls
recall her confident step, her
songbird whistles. They listen
through bee hum
for the shove of her spade,

and the cabin still resonates
with her touch on piano keys,
her frailing banjo strum.
Floorboards speak
of where she angled her desk
to catch northern cardinals
bobbing over snow.

The light-spattered porch
recollects how she cranked
open the casements
and cecropia moths blew in
to totter on the easel's wooden ledge.

Near the lake, a rock bench
warmed by a casual sun
marks the span of silence she cast,
waiting for what came
on its own accord.

My Good Fortune

Limberlost Cabin

"Yet the aggravations of fieldwork were often off-
set by better days, when good fortune seemed to
follow her."
—Judith Reick Long,
Gene Stratton-Porter: Novelist and Naturalist

I searched for it in places no lady would set foot—
in ankle-deep muck and rancid waters, a gray veil
of gnats stuck to my breath. I fought for it
on shaky ladders, near the fetid mouth of logs,
with every blind step where a mottled
massasauga could be coiled.

But other times it came to me—a quivering
whistle in the night, and all I did
was darken the room to one pale flicker
and crouch, calling back to that shadow
on an empty limb, until *Otus asio* flew through
the opened window in one tremulous sweep like the last
breath of my brother carried under by the river
but holding on past all belief
and me running yet falling further behind.

When I looked up, there it perched:
my good fortune or was it grace clasping
the back of a kitchen chair?
It turned its tufted face toward me, patient
as a priest in my stone-still house.

FIRST FLIGHT

Richmond, June 1884

It quivered in the roll and turn
as Orville banked a curve,
spun from his hubs
downhill to the river.

And a dream caught
in Will's spokes, too, as he pedaled
to the rear, reading the cursive
of turkey buzzards, how they'd

coast with wings extended,
feather-tips twisted to balance on air.
Something tugged them both
away from their mother,

wasted balsa wood thin, delicate
as the kite frames
she helped them build.
Their pockets packed

with pennies and love notes,
the ballast of loss,
they raced what snapped
at their heels—tomorrow's move

to Ohio. Under cirrus clouds,
dirt roads flew beneath them,
spokes twirled like a whirligig's
blades, like a flyer's spruce propellers

to lift them to the sky.

JAMES DEAN'S GRAVE

Park Cemetery, Fairmount

"Forty acres of oats made a huge stage, and when
the audience left I took a nap and nothing got
plowed or harrowed."

—James Dean

Where is the boy with bongo drums
and a matador's cape, with a fire-red motorcycle
racing through dust and fingers smeared
by chalk or clay?

He's not here.

He's not hovering over silk flowers and a stone
smack-full of rose-tinted kisses. He's not
fawning over cold cigarette butts or unfolding
love notes from strangers. He doesn't care
a hoot about staying where he's supposed to—lodged
among rows of graves and accessible to those
who chip and shove shards of headstone
into a purse.
             The boy who slept for years
with a piece of his mother's funeral wreath pressed
beneath his pillow would understand the need
to hold on to something, but those of you
who seek him—he's not here.

Better to fill your purses with chaff,
for he's gone into the fields, and if he's not
pounding ground with the beat
of rain, then he's riding hell-bent
over harrowed earth, stirring up dust. Or just

look for him in the solitary frame
of a farmer, shoulders slouched, hands
in his pockets, his worn boots scuffing
the crusted snow.

HELEN'S HILL

Link Observatory, Morgan County

They came to gaze at the stars,
but when Goethe Link gave his wife
a birthday bushel of bulbs, she drilled
the hard clay hill with a crowbar
so daffodils could burst into light.

As he tuned his telescope, she staked names
to her grafted blooms: *Lemon Drop*,
Towhee, *Opal Sky*. While he worked
the intricate equations of asteroids,
she multiplied earthbound constellations
by dividing the bulbs. At lunch time,
he would spread their blanket
between her beds. At night
she stood by him inside the dark dome.

After Goethe died, she buried herself
the next twenty years
in the universe of those acres,
and every April their love flares again
across Helen's hill—
a supernova that dazzles
before it fades into grass.

House of the Singing Winds

Brown County

After sunlit leaves and dove-tinted skies,
I come to the chill of a still life:
T. C. Steele's unfinished peonies
on the easel and the last dented tubes
near the stub of his Cuban cigar.

Outside, a reddish-blue haze warms
the wooded hills, but I'm drawn
to the foreground, to the forsythia
Selma planted so T. C. could paint
their cold March fire. Broad vistas

shift with light, yet I sense
restraint enfolded in a yellow shawl—
Selma's portrait in the parlor.
She's near the window, watching
what I can't see: her husband, a canvas

strapped to his back, disappearing
like a brushstroke
into the blurred trees.

POLLIE'S QUEST

"Here Pollie Barnett is at rest
From deepest grief & toilsome quest.
Her cat, her only friend,
Remained with her until life's end."
                    —Parkview Cemetery, Linton

The day her daughter disappeared
Pollie Barnett took the barnyard cat

and started striding through mud-slick
gullies and bull thistle, past

serpents that slid like thick rope
trailing an anchor. She never laced

her shoes; her overcoat flapped open
to rain, to snow. The endless

search for Sylvanie cut a fixed path
crossing five counties. Farmwives

forecast her arrival by frost or drought
or the forlorn cry of a killdeer over

a mowed field. For thirty-two years,
they gave her a pallet near their hearth

and baked the biscuits she ate
as she walked. She never gave up,

and they never told her
what an old man with his last breath

confessed. Now local girls shiver
to stories of a mournful woman

still haunting the hills. They wonder
who ties the rose to the stone cat

upon her grave. Pollie's tenacity
is in that twine—a collar of grief

that will not let go
though what it holds has already leapt

from its basket, light-footed,
into the falling snow.

DONALDSON WOODS

Spring Mill State Park

If George guarded every twig,
wasp and thistle, took potshots
at boys who'd shoot a rabbit
or scratch their name
on cave walls,

if he buried under a stone bench
the bones of a Shawnee
whose ghost lit the night
with the arc
of falling arrows,

he would only be preserving a place
where Janet could walk
in the half-light of evening,
brushing snow-on-the-mountain
to let him know she was there.

SQUIRE BOONE'S CAVERN

With Piankashaw in pursuit,
Squire stumbled on
his salvation—a leaf-plugged
sinkhole he wriggled through.
Beneath the forest floor
his heart wed water's drip
amplified by silence.

He called it holy ground
and this sibling of Daniel,
this gunsmith, brimstone preacher,
Indian fighter
who had never settled down,
built a grist mill
near the cavern spring
that rushed down the hill.

On limestone walls
where eternity inched in flowstone,
he etched verses of gratitude,
girdled them with vines.

He built his own box
from a walnut with roots knotted
at the sink edge,
and when he died, one August
Moon-when-the-cherries-turn-black,
his sons slid him
into that earthen lodge,
beneath the wild sweetgrass.

THE HARMONIST AT NIGHTFALL

Historic New Harmony
A voice from the Society of Harmonists, 1814-24

Curfew's brass bell slices through seven miles
of wilderness, past Indian mounds and my only child
asleep in an unmarked field. What if Paradise

were not a garden but a maze of trees with mottled
skin? And what if God hummed
in the cacophony we cut to lay straight streets,

to plumb brick walls? We clear bugleweed
from beds, then watch the yellow rose compose
its last notes at dusk and strive to tune our souls.

Father Rapp says death is not the cessation
of song, only the brief fermata we hold
until Christ comes again. I saw a cicada crawl out

on its resurrection morning, but it will die again.
My husband trims our pallid candles—or, rather,
my brother in Christ. If the Son of Man

rends tonight's sky with trumpet blast, He will find us fit
as that fortified chapel within our labyrinth,
each block wedged to the other and pared to a point.

Inside, Father Rapp's words inscribe the encircling wall:
"Let not the sun go down upon your wrath."
So even in dreams, scythes swing in rhythm

with the waltz. The orchestra marches us to the vineyards
and back. Our voices blend with precision as we bottle
the wine we send downriver. Not a drop sullies our lips

for we are the bride who waits by the altar and offers
long-stemmed roses to adorn heaven's iron gate.
The tight chords tether what wilts like all the rest.

GEORGE RAPP'S VISION

"The sacred task of the Harmony Society, as Rapp
intended its name to imply, was the restoration of lost
cosmic harmony in anticipation of the millennium."
—Donald E. Pitzer and Josephine M. Elliott,
New Harmony's First Utopians

It shone—a golden rose,
its petals edged
with drops of dew,
the rose Christ would pick.

We could be that rose,
I said. We could cultivate
perfection's flower
within our walled garden.

In the wilderness of Indiana,
we built a Harmonie
of such delight, pilgrims
traveled a thousand miles

to marvel at hedged
paths, a cappella hymns,
rope thick as a wrist
we'd twist from our own flax.

Celibacy was the price
we paid to keep the garden
clear of jealousy
and other bristly weeds.

But I pricked myself
on a young woman's beauty
and broke the spell
that held our harmony together.

From that wound
I bled so fiercely
every rose I touched
turned red.

John Chapman's Eden

"[He would] produce his few tattered books . . . and read and expound until his uncultivated hearers would catch the spirit and glow of his enthusiasm, while they scarcely comprehended his language."

—W. D. Haley,
"Johnny Appleseed: A Pioneer Hero,"
Harper's New Monthly Magazine, November 1871

She was upstairs with the women,
quilting rectangular blocks
into a Rail Fence.

He was sprawled by the door
in a patch of old sun,
reading the creation story
from an apple-scented bible
he carried against his heart.

Years later, she described his voice:
"loud as the roar of wind
and waves, then soft as what quivered
the morning-glory leaves
about his gray beard."

When he left,
she never closed the door
but sat in a block of sun
and stitched a path
through blackberry and cocklebur,
into a wilderness where she drank
evening's cider-hard light

and saw that the hornet was holy,
the sinuous snake fashioned
the first letter of a psalm.

LINCOLN'S FIELD

Lincoln Boyhood Memorial

He practiced the alphabet on its broken
clods, scraped with stick or toe
until what sprouted bore the snap-bean wit
of Aesop, unfurled like Arabian tales.

Thunderheads obscured the sun
when he shot a wild turkey and was struck
by a feather—a bronzed lightning
so beautiful he never brought down

another bird. Ploughing north,
he faced the cabin—turning south,
his mother's hill. To the west lay a wellspring
in the hazel; east, the road to Troy.

For fourteen years, its clay absorbed
his sorrows, fed his lanky bones.
We see it in the tin-types, the furrowed
slope of his brow.

ANTI-SLAVERY CEMETERY

Westfield

These stones have names
the rain rubs into silence: Bales,
White, Hiatt, Sumnar, Moon—Friends
of conscience who hid
the refugee behind a false
wall or their own plain
bonnet and veil, who fed
the hunter and the hunted
from the same cast iron
skillet, who led families
on foot, at night, through Dismal
Swamp, then crossed back
alone. One strayed
from his theology, raised
a stout stick to save a child.
Eleven went to war,
relinquishing
the perfection they sought.

All are gathered
in this solitary space
beneath old oak and broken
stones. All are gathered
and all are gone,
yet the Light remains
that traces the indentation
of a name.

LEVI AND CATHERINE COFFIN HOUSE

Fountain City

This house is a testament
to that which calls a man
to rise from slumber and descend
the dark stairwell, opening the door
to a blast of cold wind
and the fugitive
whose shackled, frostbit feet
he bends down
to rub near the fire.

This house is a witness
to that which moves a woman
to stoke the cast iron stove
in a kitchen below her kitchen,
to haul water from a secret well,
to make each stitch fine and tight
as if the path to freedom
might be secured
by the diligence of her needle.

And this house is a vow
given by a husband and wife
to cleave to the sacred
within the stranger, to sleep
despite threats of a hurled torch,
to enter the desperate dreams
of those who rest a fortnight in an attic,
its door hidden by the headboard
of their own bed.

THREE / MACONAQUAH'S PORTRAIT

INDIAN LAKE

"Here at a fireplace or oven on the east shore of
Indian Lake those Miamis that had comprised
Papakeecha's Band prepared their last meal be-
fore leaving tribal lands c. 1839."
                    —Roadside marker on State Road 5

    "Where is the oven?"
    my daughter says, but there is
    nothing, just a dirty white
    truck, its bed backed
    to the lake and a tattered
    stand of old cattails,
    blunt spears
    stripped of their fleece.

    Sun glints on one man
    hunched over his fishing hole,
    claiming the empty space.

    "How will he get home?"
    my daughter wonders
    as we turn to drive away,
    the solid ice receding,
    the shoreline, thin and gray.

WOLF PARK

The wolves stare with steady eyes,
old wolves with fur ragged
and gray. As we follow
the chain-link fence,
our six-year-old lags behind,
her pink rubber flip-flops
kicking up dust.

In 1838, the Potawatomi
were herded near this park,
forced to ford Tippecanoe River,
shoved up a hill
where Tecumseh's warriors
stirred, cold flames
in goldenrod.

Now the back quarter
of a buffalo vanishes
behind a wall. Tonight
people will pay
to hear the wolves howl.

One walks stiff-legged
to face my tired child,
and when she runs to catch up,
he lopes at her side.

TIPPECANOE BATTLEFIELD

~For Iona

I'm skimming William Henry
Harrison's words, how "bark

was flying from trees,"
as you linger at an empty village

preserved under glass. Who will stir
the cornmeal porridge or lift

the baby from the hummingbird
nest of a basket? If the Prophet

had waited for Tecumseh
or if Harrison had mounted

his own white horse, the Shawnee
confederacy might have won.

Outside, the smolder of Prophetstown
is just someone's uncle

lighting the grill. The white obelisk
would rise anyway, partitioning

the grass with its bayonet
shadow. But it's the boulder

with a plaque for the Potawatomi,
who years later, sick with typhoid,

trudged through this battlefield park,
you won't leave till you understand.

Why would 859 people
walk The Trail of Death to Kansas

so a single farmer could take their land?

THE PROPHET SPEAKS

"He [Tenskatawa] became everything he had once detested: a supporter of land cessions, and a dependent and instrument of the United States. . . . He was not the stuff of legend."

—John Sugden, *Tecumseh*

One-eyed and clumsy,
I was Tecumseh's ugly brother,
the one with something missing,
who built myself a pulpit
so others couldn't kick me.

I was the evangelist
who said the white man's bullets
would soften into sand,
dissipating as I danced, secluded
from the fighting. When the dust
settled, I blamed a woman
for contaminating my prayers.

I was the born-again convert
to the old ways, who exhorted
my congregation not to drink
and then, to ease my pain,
sought the solace of the bottle.

I was the priest behind the mask
who recognized the witches
by the way they ignored me.
Sloshed from whiskey, I peered
into the dirty windows of my dreams
to sketch the interior of hell.

But how can anyone say
I was not the stuff of legend?

I was more than the shadow
behind Tecumseh's shooting star.
I was the hero's spirit
in the looking glass,
who moved as he moved
but in the opposite direction.

TRADE ROUTE

White River Greenway

Wherever other girls go
on a Saturday in October,
it's *not* with their mother,
tagging along on a trail
that doesn't lead anywhere
they can Facebook their friends.

You kick hedge apples
down to the river
as I read aloud the plaque
commemorating William Conner
who traded whiskey for furs
and married Mekinges,
a Lenape chief's daughter.

Six children later, he parleyed
the tribe's removal to Kansas
and brought home his neighbor's
daughter to warm his cold hearth.

You hand me a leathery pod
with a tart lemon scent
and lead me down to the bank
where you unearth
speckled stones, chipped
snails, mother-of-pearl mussels—
the water-buffed remnants
from Mekinge's lost dowry.

MEKINGES' STORY

Before we left, I cut six sprigs
of live-forever,
the purple-flowered sedum
that roots from any broken part,
and planted them by our cabin door,
one for each child
I was taking with me.

William Conner, my husband,
grew rich on the White River,
trading liquor for Lenape furs—
then he negotiated our removal.

He rode with me that last day,
our youngest, content
in the crook of his arm.
When he turned for home,
the baby cried
and white settlers pilfered
our provisions.

William never saw the fleshy
leaves he trampled.
He married the neighbor's
blue-eyed daughter, built her
a fine brick house.

In the wilderness of his dreams,
did he enter our mud-chinked cabin
and tussle with his firstborn sons,
the ones who grew, he said,
like weeds?

MACONAQUAH'S PORTRAIT

"Francis Slocum was a patient sitter, and wholly abandoned herself to my professional require-ments."

—George Winter, 1839

Without flinching, I bore his gaze
till I became one of the Seven Pillars,
the stone bluff that banks
the Mississinewa.
                    In that dim cave
where Council met, my spirit hid
from his pencil's probe and I glimpsed
the future through Manitto's robe of rain:
the Miami herded to the white man's canal,
his brightly painted boats. Sandhill cranes
cried, their necks strained in flight
as my people shoved earth into small, sodden
bags, a keepsake of the shore.
                    He wanted to capture
my spirit, he said, so that my white brothers
would have something of a lost sister
they could keep. I knew they'd latch me
to the wall, near the long looking glass
and tiny silver spoons
they used to stir their tea.
                    My mother searched
the faces of village girls and later,
their reticent hands as she hunted
for a stub finger, part of me
that was missing. Because she was
a Quaker, acquainted with Manitto's spirit
within all things, I like to think
she found me, at last, in the sweep
of an arm, the dance
of the crane.

That is how I want you
who hear my story to find me—
not pressed to some fixed canvas,
the White Rose severed
from her stem, but among those
born with the red-crowned
cranes from the clay
bottom of the river, shattering
the surface with one great breath.

CHIEF SHIPSHEWANA

"The Chief was removed from this reservation
September 4, 1838 and was escorted to Kansas by
a company of soldiers. He returned in 1839 and
died in 1841."
—Monument inscription, Shipshewana Lake

A French priest
gave me the name *Peter the Great*,

but to the Potawatomi
I was still *Vision of a Lion*

and that was enough
to guide me back

in the dark where I met
my shadow pacing

the burnt shoreline
where the village stood.

Sycamores creaked
in their old winter bones.

I remembered
the emptiness of Kansas,

the wind with nowhere
to rest its head. I stepped

into my shadow and we
slipped where no one

could break us apart,
like otter

beneath a lodge
of ice.

SIMON POKAGON AND THE FARMER

"In the 1870's, a well-educated Indian came to Lake
County about twice each year to visit the graves of
his ancestors."
        —Kankakee Valley Historical Society

From the way he squinted
I knew that farmer had no iota
of what to make of me—
a savage in a tailored suit
who quoted Shakespeare and Tecumseh,
spoke Potawatomi and Greek.

Near juniper, I prayed
for those who cradled me. I spoke
to steady their steps down slick
ravines. I sang that their days
might be pleasant among heaven's
herds of buffalo and elk.

One April, I found the mounded
graves plowed under, shin bones
stacked with fieldstones. I could have
splashed the kerosene of a curse
but, instead, turned to offer
my grief, a treeless prairie
without periphery. Those bones
could be mine or his.

My tribe's revered flower—
the trailing arbutus—
belongs to all who observe
its delicate white blossoms
on bended knee.

As my gaze caught his,
the farmer could only clear
his throat as if pushing
away dried leaves.

FOUR / CREEKSIDE PRAYER

CREEK-SONG

It begins in a cow lane
with bees and white clover,
courses along corn, rushes
accelerando against rocks.
It rises to a teetering pitch
as I cross a shaky tree-bridge,
syncopates a riff
over the dissonance
of trash—derelict icebox
with a missing door,
mohair loveseat sinking
into thistle. It winds through green
adder's mouth, faint as the bells
of Holsteins heading home.
Blue shadows lengthen,
but the undertow
of a harmony pulls me on
through raspy Joe-pye-weed
and staccato-barbed fence.
It hums in a culvert
beneath cars, then empties
into a river that flows oboe-deep
past Indian dance ground, waterwheel
and town, past the bleached
stones in the churchyard,
the darkening hill.

AMISH HYMN

If you catch its cadence
in the night, in a slow

and somber rain,
then by Sunday morning

hoof clip will have carried
the rhythm further,

a refrain you'll follow
down a road where bullfrogs

drone bass notes
from the stiff bur-reeds

of a creek.
You're getting closer

the moment you grasp
wind's lyrics in wheat:

how nothing it touches
is ever alone. Field

meets road in a swell
of bellflowers or the rasp

of ragweed and spurge.
You're immersed

in the blue hymnbook
of the sky, in the old

wheeling of starlings
over a barn, and you know

that today is a church
with its door left ajar.

THE BARN

~For Bill and Doris Mast

The last light slants
between missing boards,
illuminating what's absent:
the Holsteins, those placid hulks
that lumbered through
evening's lilac hours,
clanking their tin bells.

The same light falls
on stillness thick with dust,
bins where cracked corn
rained, boards fitted with pegs
some immigrant hammered
to endure the storms
of another century. Precision
secures the hand-hewn girders
sheathed in bark.

Like Jacob, I could take a stone
for my pillow and see what sweeps
the dark with the curve
of its wing. But the ladders
are gone and so are the angels
who hovered near a girl
as she rolled off her stockings
to cross the high beam.

Only mud nests plastered
to ledges remain, and the swallows,
perched in the dusk.
They've been salvaging
the same notes, over and over,
earthy and sweet
as the water
we pumped from the well.

IDELLA

For one immortal summer,
she rolled off her stockings to cross
the beams girding my grandfather's barn.
She was fifteen and longed for something
she couldn't quite reach. Balancing
on a hand-hewn rafter was
nothing more than stepping out
on a limb, and the humid hour held
its breath, the sparrows fell
silent. Dust hung suspended
as she passed through shafts of light,
an austere anointing. Then
Idella coiled her braids under
a covering and took her place
in a kitchen with the tick of a clock
she had to rewind.

CREEKSIDE PRAYER

~In memory of John Mishler

By this rusty bridge rail,
where red-winged blackbirds
congregate on cattails,
my grandfather cut the engine
to hear bullfrogs thrum a chorus.

Clad in his gray suit
with the starched standup collar,
he'd take a long swig
from the earth-rimmed
jug of a Sunday morning.

His wife prodded him
to hurry, but the psalm
that moved him to prayer
rose from a wayward creek
the color of molasses.

It came from a country
so warm it made him shiver.

BUCKEYE

My grandfather carried its luck
in an overall pocket with pennies
and nails, peppermints and Tums.
It kept away rheumatism
as he rubbed the burgundy surface,
smooth as a worry stone.
The one he picked up for me
came from along the creek
where he would sleep on humid
nights in August with rustling
snakes and whip-poor-wills. Wedged
between my drainage ditch
and a privacy fence, a remnant
of wetland still survives.
One scruffy buckeye tree drips
with April blossoms, the milk glass
chips of old chimes. In autumn,
it drops its spiny pods and turns
the color of rust on a tractor
left for decades in the rain.

FARMYARD

Tonight, my uncle backs a tractor
through the dark and into a barn

no one has opened for years.
One light is on in the milk house.

One child kneels at a window
watching the wind. Only Snowball

who has died and come back
with the same name knows I am here.

He straddles his spot near the stoop,
yapping his heart out

in absolute silence. Heat lightning
strikes a match to the sky

and the garden grows thick
with what draws spirits down, incense

of pungent tomato leaves
my grandmother presses

to my palm. I am falling
into the motions of what haunts

this farmyard: flap of aprons,
lift and plunge of a handle, turn

of a crank, rush of salt, ice,
everything a dance

I want to grab hold and join.
One day, I will wake and the barn

and its dust will be swept away.
No dented dog dish. No sand

in an old tractor tire. I scoop
what's been lost beneath the hollyhocks,

hoisting it toward the backboard
my uncle fashioned from a plywood sign

that still reads "Marion Mennonite Church."
Its dim letters appear like runes

in the moonlight.

CATBIRDS

It's a blessing to catch a glimpse
of their plain feathers, the smoky
gray of slate shingles in the rain, and spy
their black eyes shining with every secret
they will never tell. They prefer
the thickest brush along the creek,
the overgrowth around an abandoned shed.
My grandfather as he lay dying
recalled the catbirds of his childhood,
how they sang mornings in the white
spirea by an empty house, as if their
hearts would break with every clear note—
their offering to the world.

THE OLD ONES

~For Nicholas Lindsay

In winter they hung in honey locust
hidden among wrinkled pods, until
spring opened their knuckles

and they bee-lined to a sprouting cornfield
where the slightest breeze set
their bird hearts humming.

On humid afternoons grown heavy
on tall stalks, they watched
for a child who moseyed near, kicking

loose gravel. They lured me inside
with a stray kitten's cry. Further
and further I wandered, past hissing

corn that grew into a forest,
and in a veil of dust I saw them,
through blue dragonflies.

When I left the dark field, rows
closed behind me in a rush. I walked
uphill toward a room where soup

had grown cold. Since then I have wondered
if the flicker of lanterns was a dream
by the curving brook. But I heard

their killdeer cries the day men cleared
the fencerow and pushed the corn under
cul-de-sacs named for what was never here.

To Fireflies in a Drought Year

Crawl out, now, from sun-struck
lawns where once you slept on moist bark

and horse-nettle, under jaunty May-apples,
their green umbrellas. Ascend in the dusk

that sealed wild sun-drops, washed
buckeyes back to the cobble-gray sea.

Come in that twilight when the croaking
of tree frogs thickened the foliage,

when chimney swifts dove into tea-scented
sycamores. Flicker, cautious spirits,

your tiny orbs of light. Mark the border
between my yard and the old, enchanted forest.

MONUMENT CITY ROAD

"How I came to that leaf-shadowed house by the
     river. . . ."
                              —Jared Carter, "Monument City"

The road, a broad, grassy path
bordered by forest, leads to a town,

and when the water is low,
they say you can see what remains.

We speak of Atlantis. Of things gone under.
I was seven, pedaling my bike

through another sleepy farm town
on the Wabash, past blue hydrangeas

and brick storefronts, some boarded up
when the dark reservoir rose

over Monument City—its rooftops,
tall, heavy elms. Now nettles

block the road. We step
where poison ivy grows thicker.

The shoreline recedes
into nightfall as the road dips

toward the black-shuttered house
where I slept in the attic.

A diner held the second-hand
smoke of old farmers. Main Street

was anchored to Methodist bells
now muffled by moss.

COVERED BRIDGE

The same space still spans the river
though there are no creaking boards
to cross, no passage through something

basking in the sun. Near its mouth
we filled plates with barbecued
chicken and 7-Up salad, and when

we drove home, lovers leaving
bottles, dark and sour, moved closer
into the dusk. Even on humid afternoons,

it was cooler by that placid curve
of the Wabash, shaded by ash
and fields away from where things

stirred. Only the rippling of water
was real, and when I peered through
the floor—where did it go, that gap

between surface and bridge? The old ones
recall how when sunlight struck
at an angle, the past reappeared:

Red Front Drug Store and *Herron's
Barber Shop,* placards interspersed
with initials of lovers plighting their troth.

Girls in white frocks who planted
easels on the bank still paint from memory
the vivid blush of the bridge and feel,

as they dip, the river's cold edge,
the distance from where they stood
and the stockings sloughed on the rocks.

Tarantella

Today cicadas strum
a ballad the bees remember
as they loiter, cider-drunk,
among the fallen apples.

It's a chorus that turns
on rickety green wheels
past frost-struck trees
whose leaves curl upward.

It's an old gypsy love song
that overwhelms the air
like the startling yellow flutter
of butterflies near a face.

It's a tune about forgetting
who you are,
of letting the wind pick
every pocket clean.

FIVE / CIRCLE CITY

On the South Step
Of Christ Church Cathedral

a prehistoric squid
is caught in pitted stone.

If you kneel, you can trace
the long, conical shell,

faint as the life line
etched upon your palms.

Close your eyes
and think of Sunday morning:

all those brisk black shoes
and stiletto heels,

tapping across the ocean floor.

WASHINGTON STREET, INDIANAPOLIS AT DUSK

Painting by Theodor Groll / 1892-95
Indianapolis Museum of Art

It's not merely that the sun
dissolves in the northeast
nor that the Statehouse broods
too near the street. Something else
is not right, and the dog with a boy
at the end of a leash
knows it. He braces hind legs
and will not budge.

Could it be the bearded man
brandishing his brass-headed
cane to hail the Blake Street
trolley who causes the dog
to bristle, this man with
a face cold and precise
as a pocket watch, who stands
oblivious to pedestrians bartering
or loitering close to the foreground,
their faces blurred with hurried
brushstrokes?

Or does the dog detect some danger
further on, past Park Theatre,
its liturgical line of hansom cabs,
the sulfuric haze
of electricity and gas?

Maybe the dog is tired. Maybe
he does not want to step
into the future,
but would rather follow
trolley tracks back
to an avenue of porches
and his own ragged rug
by the hearth.

The end of a century
and he surmises
what those looking askance
can't foresee:
when the mules turn the trolley,
they will vanish, as will
the wagons, the vendors, the fish-tainted
barrels, the scent of horse sweat
and bread.

Maybe his dog sense warns him
that from a distance
nothing matters, not
a dog, not a boy,
not a dingy street, nothing
but the ethereal theatre,
or rather, its façade,
illuminated by a light
almost lurid.

STOREFRONT PICNIC

Days Gone By Antiques

What we need is in this window: white
linens beneath a mason jar of crocus
and the straw hat propped like an afterthought
against the antique dresser. If we remove
the jar, then the wine bottle fits
inside the basket as do the olive-colored
grapes that drape a chair seat and the lemons
poised to best advantage near the empty
pitcher. Let's leave the cabbages
where they have rolled but take
the ceramic cat curled near the lantern
filled with turquoise oil.

Now to choose our spot from the painting
above the lime-green afghan meant as grass
since in this acrylic scene the ground
is almost bare. It's autumn and wind
blurs the brown and orange leaves. You thought
this was a spring or summer picnic?
So did I, but this is surely late November
unless we imagine it otherwise. Don't look
too closely or you'll see everything contorted
like our reflection in the goblet that spouts
the pitcher's brim. Nothing fits, not the straw
hat perched on your head, nor the cat
circling my lap. The sun that should be
straight above glares like the bare bulb
of the brass lamp illuminating the basket.
You should have brought that lantern
I mentioned, but let's not panic. This could be
a virtual Eden. I'll pass you an apple.
You pretend to take a bite.

NATURE'S SCHOOL

Holcomb Gardens, Butler University

Beyond the waterfall's faint trickle,
the fir trees dripping into their own reflection;
past the earbuds, cell phones, and people
pulled by dogs, the girl perusing T. S. Eliot
in the grass and the canal's arched bridge,
its honking geese; further than the beer bottle
bobbing upside down, twisted lilacs
churning with bees, stones spouting
Plato, Hegel and Locke and the bell tower
chiming "On the Banks of the Wabash,"

beyond all this—ten thousand things—
an elderly man and woman sit
turned toward each other
on a bench in the sycamore's shade.
He holds her hand as if she
were his *sweetheart Mary,*
as if he's asking once more for that hand.

Through chickadees and bumblebees
and the calliope reprise of a clock—
I overhear the renewed pledge
of lovers who have unlatched
the schoolyard gate
and stepped back to a morning
when raindrops fell on the river
and nothing they touched
had a name.

THE DEER OF CROWN HILL

To them, it's all the same—
to graze on Dillinger's grave
or the overgrowth
among the orphans. If they
leap up Riley's hill after
aspiring poets have sheathed pens
and driven home, it's not
to sense the troubadour's ghost
hovering at the crest, but because
it is a pleasure to run
so steep a slope, to savor
wind and waning sun. Who
beneath the moon would
disallow a soundless revelry
on President Harrison's roped off plot,
a lovers' gambol on the grass?
Who in heaven's name
would banish buoyant hooves
from a field chalked
with crosses? Surely
not the dead with nothing
but the machinations of memory
to occupy the hours. Moored
to his portico on the hill,
Booth Tarkington observes
the assemblage of herds
against the gold glint
of ginkgo while the Gypsy
King, dazed from a serenade
of cicadas, rises from his wagon box,
consumed by solicitude
for the moist-eyed forms
who drift through his wanton arms.

TO THE POET OF CIRCLE CITY

~In memory of Etheridge Knight (1931-1991)

Mr. Knight, you're soused again
on moonshine. You've left
a Crown Hill doorstep
to shout your free verse on Indiana Ave,
your offbeat cadence swinging
in cold rain, past the blink
of red lights. When you say, *We free singers*
be, baby / tall walkers, high steppers /
hip shakers, forlorn street corners
morph into a dance floor. You speak
no jive, black / smith who forged
your ore-block of pain
into the tongue of a bell. I'll testify
on old church bricks that your
words trumpet loose what dams
the stream. Troubadour of twisting
rivers and trees that lean into each other,
croon me another full-throated
love song, include me as kin
spliced to the green branch of your line.
Poet of the heartbeat, you were no
square scribe but a line-
breaker, music-maker, who set
every circle humming—plum, moon,
lake, star—till in the midst of life
you tripped, bereft
of breath. But the saucers still
spin on their sticks and you,
touch-tender muse / father,
still tell us that *freedom's place*
is neither ahead nor behind / Neither
right nor left. The world is round.
And 'round the Circle we ride.
Your free-song swings
on wheels that kiss the earth and
turn on a silver dime.

HARD TRUTHS: THE ART OF THORNTON DIAL

Indianapolis Museum of Art, 2011

We went to learn how a black man
who welded Pullman cars and fixed

water pipes under the asphalt in Alabama
made art that spoke of freedom.

Back at the community center in our
makeshift circle of chairs, we discussed

his carousel of lost cows—skeletons
orbiting a leather golf bag—and his sky

crammed with paint cans split open
into stars. The students turned off

their iPods and hunkered down
to make poetry from their own hard

streets where people say, "Shake what your
momma gave you" and gunshots puncture

the night. They used what they knew
and hammered it into hip-hop.

They found rags snagged on barbed wire
and gave them wings to fly.

They soldered a voice to broken
Barbies and teddy bears stained red.

They built something to last
from the petals of shredded tires

and the glint of bottle glass.

AT THE SCHOOL FOR THE BLIND

~For Bonnie Maurer

"Poetry is a river,"
the boy says, his fingers
touching the rippled

surface. A girl peers through
the thick lens of her glasses,
reaches to untie

the dinghy from a dream
that transports us
over forest. It's natural

as a dance—how students
guide each other
to the microphone

and back. So many forays
from this brick castle
to the canyon behind the hills

where the sun stables
its team of light-footed horses
and sleeps

under a thin blanket
of stars.

GRAY MORNING AT FOUNTAIN SQUARE

"I could make you a snake, a lizard
or a Bengali tiger," says the woman painting

faces near the fountain. This is the first
morning of fall, the day of equilibrium,

but it's so overcast, even adults
dish out for chartreuse scales. Sidewalk artists

spread blue tarps to catch stray
splatters of paint, and behind a weathered

pew in Arthur's Music Store,
red, pink, yellow and brown guitars

line up like a fervent, righteous choir.
On Woodlawn Avenue, Rose of Sharon

hedge out the interstate. I leaf
through hand-tinted postcards of Paris.

"Good morning, young lady,"
an old man says, though I am almost fifty.

"Good morning," with a lilt that balances
sunshine and rain, darkness and light.

FESTIVAL OF COLOR

India Community Center

We scoop green, pink and saffron
powder from platters broad as the Purnima
Moon and dance into the havoc of Holi,
back to our youth, when chalk festooned
concrete as now color leaps from a fist
into this overcast sky, coating hair, face,
suit and sari until we are born again
from the dust of flowers.

BAISAKHI

~For K.P. and Jan Singh
Baisakhi is an Indian harvest festival, a Punjabi new year
celebration and a commemoration of the founding of the
Khalsa (Sikh brotherhood) in 1699.

Dancers drive oxen with the flick
of a wrist. The smooth sweep

of their unseen scythes wing
through winter wheat. A bride,

resplendent in red, rushes to the groom
who has died in her arms

a hundred times before.
We're in Indianapolis, but in this dim

crowded room where the face
of an old man radiates more light

than the halogen globe behind him,
I'm a pilgrim in the Punjab,

eating rice and curried goat with a friend
who says we've all been here before

and that's the source of so much fervor,
I feel it in hands that hold on longer

than a handshake. Drums draw
children to the stage, everyone else

to a floor that blossoms with Sikh turbans,
kurtas and scarves. In a beat that bounds

without sense of time beyond the circle,
no one bows to just one partner

but to the divine spark within.

Six / Sylvan Springs

OLD QUARRY

McCormick's Creek State Park

I.

Once, a railroad was here
and a pit where men blasted rock
and roped it, where the sun
burnt their bent necks
as they chiseled blocks
to make the Statehouse.

They swigged bitter coffee
from canteens and ate
sandwiches on the stumps
of white oak toppled
for whiskey barrel staves.

II.

A hundred years later
what remains is a ruin
in the forest, rain-scoured,
splotched with moss.

At dusk, the stagnant pond
shines with amber light
and shadows carve
the cavorting figures
of foreign gods.

THE LERNER THEATRE, 1953

Elkhart

When my mother purchased high heels
at Ziesel's Department Store
and then crossed Main Street
toward a white terra cotta wall
with a marquee that announced,
From Here to Eternity,
it was the beginning of the end.

When she fell head over heels in love,
not just with Burt Lancaster, loping,
bare-chested across the beach,
but with the click of her blue
stilettos on terrazzo stone,
it was the end of the world
as a good Mennonite knew it.

The girl who made a necklace
from safety pins to wear
beneath her dress to school
marveled at the extravagance
of beaded chandeliers. She saw
dancing maids and griffins,
pipes, harps and Grecian urns,
the Turkish screens behind box seats,
the plush gold, pleated curtain.

All of it was worldly.
All of it was good.

Outside, the city was an oven,
but she slouched in a sanctuary
cooled by the river's pumped water
sprayed as fine mist into fans.

She loitered with hundreds of other sinners
in a dome of darkness

where she could see distinctly
the complications
a romantic life could take.

There she was: on the deck
with Deborah Kerr, tossing
her lei upon Pearl Harbor,
watching a wave, like a cursive swirl,
sweep the flowers out to sea.

WEST BADEN SPRINGS HOTEL

It's the moment before Vesuvius
and Mr. Sinclair stands beneath his opulent dome,
checking a gold pocket watch
one last time while Lillian's collie
whines at his feet, alert to some small
sound, the shuffling of cards or the chauffeur
pulling the chrome handle on Al Capone's
black Lincoln. It's before Capone steps out
and Joe Louis leaves for the side of town
where women who take in laundry toil
over lingerie edged with exquisite lace.
Irving Berlin whistles a snatch of what will be
"Alexander's Ragtime Band," a boutonniere
on his lapel. The vender, a girl
from French Lick, sees her violets wilt
in the sun that beats on the words,
"Carlsband of America."

Somewhere the click of dice,
someone wagers all he has that fate tips
her fan in his favor. But in the atrium,
stone muses are stoic, ready to endure
the rain of hot ash. Without shifting an eye,
they watch the skirts that swish and inch
upward, ruffles, plush hats, flirtatious
red feathers. A silent film star with insomnia
and female complaints presses her lips
to the rim of a glass and prays for the waters
to heal her. That's what they all ask,
though not in so many words. It's the hope
of the draw or the fear that their bluff
will be called, the glitter rub off in the wash.

Lillian falls asleep for hundreds of years
and wakes to find her husband a scoundrel
as fake as his spats. It's before she leaves
with the soldier who fought for breath
in the trenches, before her father dies
and the collie lies buried beneath the atrium floor.
Vanderbilts still stroll serene sawdust paths

and silver rings on crystal as John L. Sullivan
clears his palate with pineapple sherbet. The milk-fed
capon sizzles in its broth. Electric lights blaze.

When the Market crashes, it's the collapse
of the cards: the guests fold what they have
and go home before white flakes of silence
darken the dome, cover Apollo's Spring, fill
the Italianate fountain. The Jesuits come
with books and black robes to buy Pompeii
for a buck.

MOTHER GUERIN SPEAKS
OF A CHAPEL BUILT OF SHELLS

St. Mary-of-the-Woods College

In gratitude for the shift of wind
that set our ship aright
when a storm's leviathan wave
had flipped it beam end down,
the Sisters and I built Shell Chapel
with what we found in the Wabash River.

If the Sisters of Providence whispered
that my vision was excessive, I never
overheard. Shoveling mussels,
I listened for an echo of my childhood
on Bretagne's granite coast where I collected
pierced scallops to bead
for rosaries and bits of bottle rubbed
into stained glass. I'd tilt
those tiny windows, delicate as thumbnails
or fish scales, to watch for my father's
merchant ship, bearing sacks of turmeric
and ginger, reams of silk.

The Sisters and I plastered snails
to form planks of the clipper
that brought me to where I stood—
in an Indiana wilderness I never wanted,
where food supplies and books were scarce
and the bishop in Vincennes drew
his purse strings tight.

Just as I began to sink,
Christ walked upon the Wabash
and ringed my finger with mother-of-pearl
dredged from its mud floor.
He taught me to fathom the queries
in my students' eyes and to mark the current
rising in the cottonwood. When I'd leave
the dim conch of the chapel, asters

and sun-drops lapped a shoreline
so dazzling it would blind me.

I was buried, as I requested,
near the chapel door, but now
that I'm canonized, they've dug up my bones
to lay beneath a vaulted roof braced
by marble columns. You can murmur
a prayer as you brush the polished lid,
but to listen to my voice, come
to the chapel built with the hinged shells
creatures like me were pulled from.

With my Sisters, I sing
how grace is a provident ocean, taking our breath
and bringing it back—from graveyard bottom
to this forest arched with stars.

FROM THE FOUR DIRECTIONS

St. Paul Catholic Center, Bloomington

When the Tibetan monks enter,
I remember a red barn

where Amish intoned hymns
old as the long, bass horns

calling us to the black
grotto of a breath. Smoke

from a Shoshone pipe
blesses each direction. Pungent

clouds of incense spread
a saffron sunrise.

"*We* and *They* are no longer here,"
the Dalai Lama says, floating

a white silk scarf.

SYLVAN SPRINGS

Rome City

After the others drive away,
I splash my face with water
from the fount that dried up
just before the Sisters sold their sanitarium
to a bible college cult
that boarded up stained glass windows
and lowered the ceilings.

I drink deeply from the metallic-tasting
draft that started flowing
thirty years later
on a Good Friday afternoon.

I want to believe
water cured consumptive coughs
and now whatever plagues the pilgrims
entering the overgrown gardens
through the open gate: arthritis,
leukemia, the unexplained pressure
behind the eyes
of a man who'd never heard
of Sylvan Springs till he
descended its crumbling stairs,
instructed in a dream.

I trace the faded lines
of shuffleboard on cement
and hope a benefactor comes forward
who starts the boilers that heat the pipes
and restores the ornate tin ceilings,
the guest rooms filled with fresh-cut flowers.

I pray someone saves Mercy Chapel
without carting casino tables across
the floor where Sister Mildred Neuzil knelt
when Our Lady tapped her shoulder,
cradling the world in one arm.

I cross the bridge
over soft continents of algae
and take the trail to Holy Family Hill, past
a stone grotto filled with folding chairs
and the field of asters and nettle
where Sisters grazed their Guernseys.

At the top, Mary and Joseph gaze down;
each touch their young son's shoulder.
Joseph clasps a staff sprouting
resurrection lilies, while Jesus raises
his fingers in a peace sign. He's looking

past me, into the firs
where I glimpse the silken ears
and dappled backs of two half-grown deer.
I walk closer as they step further
down and edge back, not daring to blink
as if they can't believe
what has appeared above the crest,
out of ordinary air.

PRELUDE

Serenity Restaurant, Zionsville

My daughter and I are savoring
a thick slice of chocolate ganache cake

garnished with cream as the Turkish samovar
disappears, along with the tin-punched

pie safe and the salt and pepper swans.
"We need forty-two of everything,"

a voice calls out from the kitchen.
Then the rumble of crushed ice,

the bright click of crystal. We surmise
there's a wedding tonight in this

Victorian house where we pour
almond tea amidst vanishing tables.

Mahogany chairs take their places
to face what ends in baby's breath

and peach roses. We divide
the last scone beneath a tin ceiling

wreathed like a cake. Soon
harp strings will ripple. The bride

will listen for her cue and glance
at the clock, its pendulum spoon.

"It's time to go," my daughter says,
stacking the china. She scoots back

and waits while I finish what's left
of my tea, the flavor of marzipan.

THE SUNKEN GARDENS

Huntington
~In memory of Perry and Lucile Miller

"Winding paths lead near cool waters and masses
of bloom, in the place made out of a dream."
   —*Better Homes and Gardens*, November 1929

Poised on this limestone bridge, gray now,
but then it shone white, Lucile still wears

her bridal corsage, orchids pinned
to a stiff tailored suit. They have come,

like the others, to gaze into their melded
shadows, where goldfish, like shards

of stained glass, glide. They marvel
at beds of begonias and swirling

iris bordered by coleus. If paradise
can be hewn from the raw gape

of a quarry, then the years will only add
more layers of bloom. They cannot see

how this radiance fades and negligence
mows the flowers, vandals seize the rest.

Stone, water, grass. That's all
that remains, the bare geometry

of a garden when memory has eroded
its own lush bank. This algae-covered

pond has no bottom but mud
and more mud, but that can't be true,

and though you both wander
through a maze of beige hallways

and can't reach each other, there must
be a place where you meet.

Maybe it's here—on this bridge—
where traffic is muffled by maple leaves

miles above what matters in a life
immortalized by the sudden

brush of a kiss.

The Prayers of Saint Meinrad

For more than a century, prayers like snowflakes
have been falling. They drift across the hillside

and melt on each station of the cross. They cover
graves where monks rest beneath Gregorian chants,

touch the spires of the abbey, soak
into its sandstone walls. Vespers sweep

through a corridor, past framed photographs
of priests, to bank near St. Benedict

with his devoted crow and a gentle St. Meinrad,
his bare foot restraining the Devil's fuming head.

In the Chapter Room upstairs, a Belgian monk's
passionate entreaties still sting like a blizzard

descending from the ceiling he painted
as World War II stoked its ovens. His supplications

appeal to Christ's own book—*Ergo Sum Vita,*
"Hence, I Am Life." They fall swiftly from scaly,

underwater creatures, from bright beasts of the jungle,
from every sign of the zodiac swirling

in God's night sky.

LAST PILGRIMAGE

Pine Hills Nature Preserve

I will go, when I am old,
to a box canyon
where ice and water
have chiseled the earth
down to its bones.

I will touch my youth
in the blue shadows
of Honeycomb Rock
and in the emptiness
where a mill once stood,
its waterwheel turning
in my head.

I will quiet that wheel.

Then walk into the white hive
of a dream some glacier
pulled down from the North
and balance in the silence
on Devil's Backbone,
a hundred feet above
two creeks sidewinding
toward each other.

On that smooth spine
I'll kneel among etchings
of passenger pigeons
engraved when clouds
of their bodies swept
through the sky.

I'll listen for their wings,
sleigh bells mixed
with thunder.

THE AUTHOR

Shari Miller Wagner was born in Goshen, Indiana and grew up near Markle, a small town along the Wabash River, in Wells and Huntington Counties. Her father worked as a family physician and her mother as the editor of *The Markle Times*. When Wagner was thirteen, her family spent a year in Somalia, in the village of Jamama, where her father served as the only doctor at a Mennonite hospital.

After majoring in English at Goshen College, Wagner worked in Louisiana as a Mennonite volunteer for the Clifton-Choctaw, researching the tribe's history and tutoring the school children. Later, at Indiana University, she studied poetry in the MFA program where she met her husband, Chuck Wagner, another student in the program. After they graduated, they taught two years at Western Carolina University and then returned to Indiana, teaching as adjuncts at Franklin College and Butler University. Over the years, she has taught creative writing in elementary schools, community centers, libraries and nursing homes. She has been an instructor with the Indiana Writers Center for the last six years, teaching workshops in poetry and memoir.

The Harmonist at Nightfall is Wagner's second book of poems. *Evening Chore* was her first, published by Cascadia Publishing House in 2005. She also co-wrote her father Gerald Miller's memoir, *A Hundred Camels: A Mission Doctor's Sojourn and Murder Trial in Somalia* (Cascadia, 2009) and was editor of *Returning: Stories from the Indianapolis Senior Center* (INwords, 2012). She has been awarded two Creative Renewal Fellowships from the Arts Council of Indianapolis, and her poems have been published in many places, including *The Writer's Almanac with Garrison Keillor* and *Best American Nonrequired Reading, 2013*.

The author, her husband and two daughters, Vienna and Iona, live north of Indianapolis in Westfield, a town founded by North Carolina Quakers in 1834. They all enjoy hiking Indiana trails and visiting the state's magnificent caves. Turkey Run, with its deep sandstone canyons, is their favorite state park.

ACKNOWLEDGMENTS CONTINUED

I wish to thank the editors of the following magazines where these poems, or their earlier versions, first appeared:

The Christian Century: "Catbirds," "Creekside Prayer," "Creeksong," "Idella" ("Daredevil") and "Olin Lake"; *Christianity and Literature:* "Amish Hymn" ("Amish Prayer"), "The Old Ones" and "Tarantella"; *The Flying Island:* "The Deer of Crown Hill"; *Friends Journal:* "The Levi and Catherine Coffin House"; *Goshen College Broadside:* "Donaldson Woods" ("The Bower"); *Maize:* "West Baden Springs Hotel"; *The Mennonite:* "Farmyard" and "Old Barn"; *The Mid-America Poetry Review:* "Clifty Falls"; *The Midwest Quarterly:* "Calling the Crows"; *The National Wetlands Newsletter:* "Rapture"; *The North American Review:* "Cataract Falls" and "Last Pilgrimage"; *Perspectives:* "The Prayers of St. Meinrad" and "Indian Lake"; *Poem in Your Pocket*, The Writers Center of Indiana: "Festival of Color"; *Poetry East:* "Buckeye" and "Helen's Hill"; *Poetry on the Buses*, Arts Council of Indianapolis: "At the School for the Blind"; *Rhubarb:* "John Chapman's Eden"; *Shenandoah:* "These Rocks"; *SikhSpectrum.com Quarterly:* "Baisakhi"; *So It Goes: The Literary Journal of the Kurt Vonnegut Memorial Library:* "Simon Pokagon and the Farmer"; *The Sow's Ear Poetry Review:* "Inside Stone," "The Soloist" and "Winter Solstice"; *Tipton Poetry Journal:* "Hard Truths: The Art of Thornton Dial," "House of the Singing Winds" and "To the Fireflies in a Drought Year"; *Traces Magazine of Indiana and Midwestern History:* "Lincoln's Field"; *Valparaiso Poetry Review:* "First Flight" and "The Naturalist."

"Simon Pokagon and the Farmer" was reprinted in the *Best American Nonrequired Reading, 2013* (Houghton Mifflin). "Anti-Slavery Cemetery" and "Washington Street, Indianapolis, at Dusk" were anthologized in *And Know This Place: Poetry of Indiana* (Indiana Historical Society Press, 2011). Earlier versions of "The Birders of Cool Creek," "Covered Bridge," "James Dean's Grave," "The Sunken Gardens" and "West Baden Springs Hotel" appeared in *Evening Chore*, (Cascadia Publishing House, 2005). "The Sunken Gardens" first appeared in the anthology, *A Cappella: Mennonite Voices in Poetry* (University of Iowa Press, 2003).

BOTTOM DOG PRESS

BOOKS IN THE HARMONY SERIES

The Harmonist at Nightfall: Poems of Indiana
By Shari Wagner, 114 pgs. $16
Painting Bridges: A Novel
By Patricia Averbach, 234 pgs. $18
Ariadne & Other Poems
By Ingrid Swanberg, 120 pgs. $16
The Search for the Reason Why: New and Selected Poems
By Tom Kryss, 192 pgs. $16
Kenneth Patchen: Rebel Poet in America
By Larry Smith, Revised 2nd Edition, 326 pgs. Cloth $28
Selected Correspondence of Kenneth Patchen,
Edited with introduction by Allen Frost, Paper $18/ Cloth $28
Awash with Roses: Collected Love Poems of Kenneth Patchen
Eds. Laura Smith and Larry Smith
With introduction by Larry Smith, 200 pgs. $16

* * * *

HARMONY COLLECTIONS AND ANTHOLOGIES

d.a.levy and the mimeograph revolution
Eds. Ingrid Swanberg and Larry Smith, 276 pgs. $20
Come Together: Imagine Peace
Eds. Ann Smith, Larry Smith, Philip Metres, 204 pgs. $16
Evensong: Contemporary American Poets on Spirituality
Eds. Gerry LaFemina and Chad Prevost, 240 pgs. $16
America Zen: A Gathering of Poets
Eds. Ray McNiece and Larry Smith, 224 pgs. $16
Family Matters: Poems of Our Families
Eds. Ann Smith and Larry Smith, 232 pgs. $16

Bottom Dog Press, Inc.
PO Box 425/ Huron, Ohio 44839
Order Online at:
http://smithdocs.net/BirdDogy/BirdDogPage.html

RECENT BOOKS BY BOTTOM DOG PRESS

CPSIA information can be obtained
at www.ICGtesting.com
Printed in the USA
FFOW02n1524150616
25052FF